Industry

Rupert Matthews

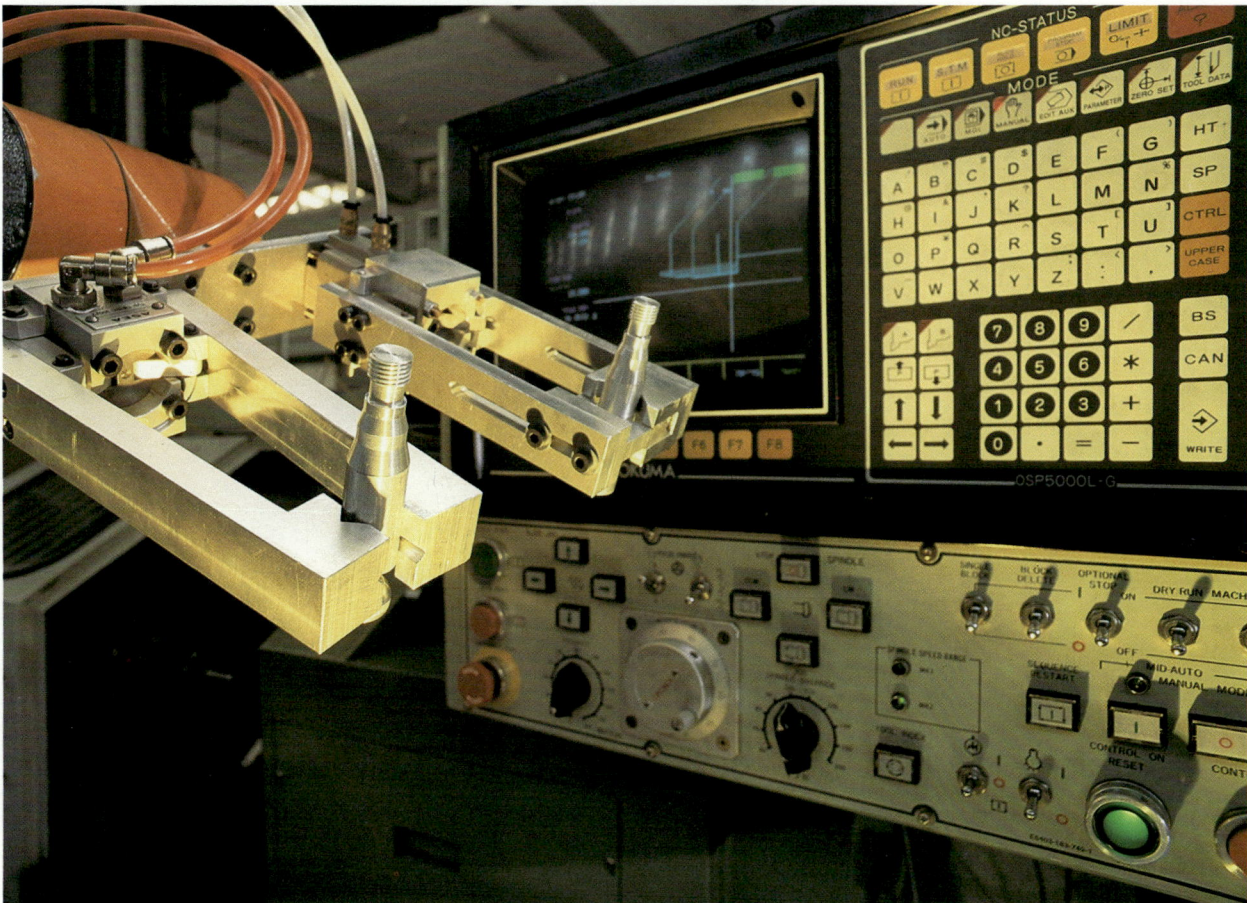

Wayland

20th Century

Titles in this series

Art
Cinema
Communications
Farming
Fashion
Industry
Medicine
Music
Science
Sport
Transport
Warfare

Editor: David Jollands

Designer: Ross George

Front cover *Spot-welding by robot in a modern car factory.*
Back cover *Women at work in a machine shop at the turn of the century.*
Frontispiece *A modern robot arm in front of the computer that controls it.*

First published in 1989 by
Wayland (Publishers) Ltd
61, Western Road, Hove
East Sussex, BN3 1JD, England

British Library Cataloguing in Publication Data
Matthews, Rupert
Industry. – (20th century)
1. Industrial development, 1900–1987 – (20th century)
I. Title II. Series
338.09'04

ISBN 0–85078–923–0

Typeset by Lizzie George, Wayland (Publishers) Ltd
Printed by G. Canale and C.S.p.A., Turin, Italy
Bound by Casterman, S.A., Belgium

Contents

Traditional Industries

The twentieth century has seen the most dramatic growth in industry. In 1900, the industrial world was largely controlled by four major powers, Britain, France, Germany and the USA. These nations drew their industrial power from the traditional or staple industries established and developed in the eighteenth and nineteenth centuries.

The nature of industry

Below The busy cotton mills at Lowell in Massachusetts, USA. Cotton was one of the major industries of the late nineteenth century.

Industry can be defined as human activity which produces objects for sale that have been manufactured from a selection of raw materials. Manufacture means literally making by hand, so a carpenter who buys materials, makes them into a chair and then sells it for more than the materials cost, is engaging in industry for profit. Some industries are carried out by people working on their own. Others demand large work centres or factories. One of these activities is shipbuilding. Hundreds of people are needed to build a large ship. These people are employed by a

company and they work in a shipyard. Industry can include manufacturing processes involving a single worker or hundreds of workers.

At the beginning of the twentieth century industry was very unevenly spread throughout the world. Four countries, Britain, France, Germany and the USA were between them producing more than 75 per cent of all industrial goods. Most other countries had agricultural economies. This means that the people concentrated on growing food to eat themselves or to sell to others. Some of this food was processed in agricultural industries, such as cheese-making and flour-milling, but most people worked on farms and made a living from the land.

In a few countries, farmers did not grow food for themselves at all but produced what are known as cash crops. In Indonesia, for instance, many farmers planted rubber trees on their land. The rubber was then sold to European companies for cash. With this money the farmers were able to buy all the food they wanted, together with extra goods such as expensive clothes or furniture. Most of the world had an almost entirely agricultural or cash-crop economy.

Above Iron and coal were the backbone of British industry in the nineteenth century. This Victorian painting portrays a typical scene of men working in a Northumbrian shipyard.

The industrial scene

Even in those countries that were industrialized, the industries were much simpler than today. The industrial scene in Britain, for example, was dominated by what were known as staple industries. These 'staples' included coal, iron and steel, chemicals, textiles and engineering. They employed millions of people and dominated the economy.

Coal-mining was one of the earliest industries to become important. In 1900 Britain produced about 230 million tonnes of coal, whereas just 50 years earlier only 86 million tonnes had been produced. The coal was burnt in steam engines to provide power for many other processes and so was vital to industrial prosperity. Iron and steel was also booming with a production of 5 million tonnes, compared with 1/2 million tonnes in 1870. Much of the steel went to feed heavy engineering, which included such things as shipbuilding and railway construction. Textile manufacture concentrated on cotton and woollen fabrics. These were produced in large mills, each employing hundreds of workers. The finished clothing was put together by individual workers, many of whom worked in their own homes.

However, the dominance of staple industry was beginning to be challenged in the more advanced countries. As greater numbers of people earned money in industry, they wanted things to spend their extra money on. This demand led to a slow rise in the production of consumer goods, which people often bought for home decoration or for their sheer novelty. In many cases such goods were still being made by individual craftsmen. However, the engineering industry was becoming more advanced and slowly introduced methods of mechanizing consumer industries. New inventions and the introduction of new techniques gave those with mechanical skills the opportunity to expand their workshops into quite large factories. This became the basis of the light-engineering industry.

In 1900, consumer industries were of minor importance. Nevertheless, some signs of their coming dominance was evident. The recent invention of the man-made fibre, rayon, threatened to displace cotton and wool as the most important textile raw materials. Other artificial cloths followed, but even by 1914 they had only a small market share.

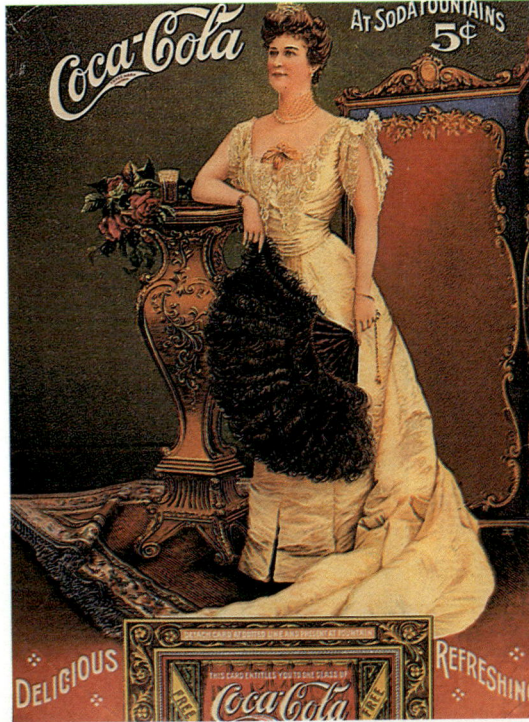

Left An advertisement for Coca-Cola dating from the 1900s. Food processing was one of the new industries providing work at this time.

Below A traditional view of heavy industry at the Cammell Laird shipyard in Scotland.

New forms of transport

Also making their appearance at about this time were new forms of transport which were to be very important for the future of industry. These were based upon the internal combustion engine which had been invented towards the end of the nineteenth century. The production of motor vehicles of all kinds quickly became a major industry. The aeroplane, however, remained unimportant for some years. The first aeroplane to be fitted with an internal combustion engine was built by the Wright brothers in the USA and made the first powered flight in 1903. However, aeroplanes were dangerous and difficult to fly and for the next decade flying remained little more than a hobby for the adventurous.

The first motor car had been built in Germany in 1885, but even in 1900 motor cars remained an expensive and unreliable form of transport. Only a few rich people had cars, but the situation was to change rapidly. In 1903, the famous engineer Henry Ford founded the Ford Motor Company. He was determined to make motor cars that were cheap enough for the mass of the American people.

In order to do this Henry Ford introduced a process known as 'the production line'. He arranged his factory so that each new car progressed slowly along a moving line. As a car passed each worker, that worker would do a single job to the car, such as fixing on the steering wheel. The car would then move on to the next worker who would do a different job. The speed of the production line was carefully controlled so that it allowed exactly the correct amount of time for each job to be done. The process was so efficient that Henry Ford was able to produce many more new cars at much cheaper prices than any other manufacturer. Within a few years the Ford Motor Company was the third largest manufacturer in the USA.

Above Around 1910 motor cars appeared on the roads and a few aircraft were flying. The Blackburn monoplane and the Peugeot car were typical.

Left Horsedrawn and motor vehicles seen alongside each other in the City of London.

New technologies

The production line was shown by Ford to be so economic and efficient that many other industries adopted it for the mass production of products that needed to be assembled from a variety of components. As a new technology, the production line was to prove its worth in the First World War which was about to begin.

In 1900, electricity, too, was a new technology and was beginning to be used in numerous industries. In 1875 the first electric telephone had been invented by a Scotsman, Alexander Graham Bell, and in 1879 the first electric light bulb was made in the USA by Thomas Edison. These and other electrical devices were beginning to be produced by industry in advanced countries for many different domestic and industrial purposes.

Above Guglielmo Marconi, an Italian, with radio apparatus similar to the equipment he used for sending and receiving the first wireless signal across the Atlantic.

Left One of Thomas Edison's original telephones. Radio and the telephone led to the development of new industries.

9

The First World War

In 1914, Austria attacked Serbia and other European nations were quickly involved. Soon Germany, Austria and Turkey were fighting against Britain, France and Russia. The USA later joined Britain against Germany. This short period of four years demonstrated that 'war' is a powerful agent for technological change. During this period, most technologies made major advances.

Industry and the war

Most people expected the war to be over very quickly, but after a year of fighting it became clear that the struggle would continue for some time. The war had a profound effect on the world economy. Governments took over control of many of their industries. In Britain, the government decided that less important kinds of manufacturing should be cut back in order to concentrate more resources on essential war industries.

Many engineering factories were converted to making guns and ammunition. Textile factories were soon turning out uniforms for the armed forces. Steel helmets, mess tins and bayonets were soon being made by small factories whose peacetime occupation was the manufacture of domestic and kitchen equipment. Some businesses gained from their government contracts and were able to make large profits.

The need for increased efficiency led governments to spend more money on research. The aircraft industry, for instance, expanded rapidly during this time, and as each side called for more and better aircraft than their opponents, vast sums of money were spent on research to upgrade designs and improve performance. In 1914 aircraft flew at about 60 kph and could carry just one man. By 1918 speeds of 200 kph were possible and bombers could lift loads of 300 kg.

However, industries not directly involved with the war suffered. They were stripped of workers and investment, causing factories to run down and machinery to wear out. Government controls meant that the 'new' industries suffered more than the well-established industries. The smooth growth of the economy was interrupted.

Below A Coventry ironworks used for the manufacture of heavy guns, called howitzers, for the army.

Left The Sopwith aircraft works in Surrey 1918. During the First World War the aircraft industry advanced rapidly.

Below A British plane attacks a German airfield in northern France.

Women in industry

Above *While young men were at war, women worked in munitions factories.*

Below *Bundling belts and braces for the soldiers.*

The war also affected the industrial work-force. Millions of men left home to fight and were killed or injured. As a result there were many jobs with no men to fill them and women moved into industry in large numbers to fill the gap. Previously, only a few women had worked in the light industries, but now they were needed in munitions factories and engineering works. Though the work was exhausting and the hours were long, the women were well paid and felt they were helping the war effort.

When the men returned after the war, most women gave up their industrial jobs. However, the experience had shown women that they could do work which earned high wages and in the years ahead more and more women were to work in light manufacturing industries, thereby increasing productivity.

The effects of war

The Great War had an effect in countries far from the scene of fighting. Because the major powers were concentrating all their efforts on the war industries, they were no longer able to maintain all their trading relationships with other countries. In some cases this caused much hardship. The farmers and craftsmen of the smaller countries were unable to trade their produce for the raw materials and machinery they needed. Many of the smaller countries fell into debt and their economies ceased to grow.

Elsewhere, however, the breakdown of trade with Europe and the USA helped some local economies to expand. When a country could no longer sell its raw materials abroad, it began processing and manufacturing goods at home. The lack of imports encouraged home-based industries to develop and become more efficient. In 1914, Japan had already started to industrialize and during the war manufacturing expanded, laying the foundations for their future prosperity.

Perhaps the most important effects of the war upon industry were the far-reaching advances that had taken place in various technologies. During the four years of war, wireless telegraphy, transport, medical and chemical technologies, and science itself had made spectacular advances. These were to shape the world of the future.

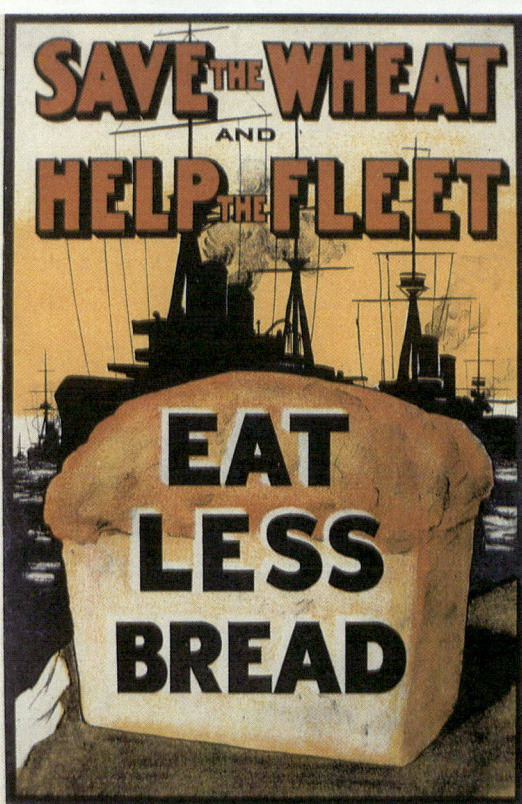

Above A British battleship steams through the Straits of Gibraltar in 1915. Many ships were sunk or damaged during the war, keeping the shipyards busy.

Left A British poster urging food economy since wheat had to be imported from other countries.

Boom and Slump

When peace returned in 1918, the world wanted to revert to pre-war prosperity as quickly as possible. Everyone thought that it would be fairly simple to return to the financial and industrial situation which had existed before 1914. But the war had drastically altered the world's economy.

Above A poster showing a passenger liner steaming through the Suez Canal. Soon after the war many people left Europe to work in Australia.

A war-shattered world

In the countries which were already heavily industrialized, effort had been concentrated on war materials such as ships, guns and ammunition. These used large quantities of the staple products such as steel and coal. As a result, large new works had been built to satisfy these demands. When peace returned there was a short boom as materials were needed to repair wartime losses and to catch up in neglected manufactures. For instance, large numbers of merchant ships had been sunk during the war and needed to be replaced. This caused a short-term rise in shipbuilding. When this demand ceased, the industries found themselves producing more than they could sell.

These staple industries had been expanded at the expense of 'new' industries, such as electrical appliance and motor car manufacture. Peace brought about a demand for these goods which could not easily be met. There were not nearly enough factories producing domestic electrical goods at cheap prices to satisfy public demand.

Investment had been channelled into the wrong industries during and immediately after the war. Coal mines, shipyards and heavy engineering works were capable of producing far more than they could sell. The money tied up in mining machinery was not available to be invested in chemical works, which would have been more profitable and useful.

Declining prosperity

This imbalance of investment and capacity caused a sudden slump in 1921. A slump is a severe fall in trade. Many companies were forced to close down and people were out of work. It was a time of hardship for workers and employers alike as business failed. Before the First World War there had been several such slumps. These had only lasted a short time and business had recovered quite rapidly afterwards. In 1921 people thought that this would happen again so they were not very worried. In fact recovery might have followed quickly as the new industries slowly expanded, but severe financial difficulties followed the slump and set the world on an economic decline.

Germany and the Austrian Empire had been defeated in the First World War. As a result these nations were heavily in debt and faced economic difficulties. To make matters worse, the Austrian Empire had been broken up into several separate countries, including Czechoslovakia, Yugoslavia and Hungary. This disrupted the easy flow of goods in south-eastern Europe, especially in the Danube Basin. Trade and industry were affected by the political changes.

Germany was not divided, but was forced to pay vast sums of money to other countries in order to pay for all the damage which her armies had caused during the war. The financial strain of repairing its own war damage, and paying for everyone else's as well, proved to be too much for Germany. The country's entire economic structure collapsed. In 1914 one US dollar had been worth 4 German marks. By 1921 one dollar bought 270 marks. This showed that economic decline was well advanced. However, the situation rapidly worsened. By November 1923 the mark had collapsed to such an extent that one dollar was the equivalent of 4,200,000,000,000 marks. People in Germany almost stopped using money, which was now virtually worthless. Workers were paid by being given food or clothing instead of money.

Above The new and rapidly growing telephone industry provided work for many people, especially women.

Left The launch of a German oil tanker in Hamburg, in 1932. By this time shipbuilding was recovering from the slump which had dominated the 1920s.

The Great Depression

The virtual removal of Germany and south-eastern Europe from international trade was catastrophic. Instead of buying goods from other countries, much of Europe stagnated. Britain and the USA had no markets for their products and the slump deepened. Drastic financial action by the USA managed to repair some of the damage caused in Europe, but not all.

In 1929 the American Stock Exchange on Wall Street suddenly crashed. The fact that this followed the other disasters resulted in an almost total collapse of international trade. All over the world millions of people were thrown out of work, and factories were closed.

Above *British miners leaving the colliery in the 1920s. Many mines were forced to close during the Depression.*

Left *A New York businessman desperately tries to raise money after the Wall Street Crash of 1929.*

This era became known as the Great Depression. In Britain, more than a quarter of the working population were unemployed. The British government paid out unemployment pay, known as the dole, and free food was handed out at 'soup kitchens'.

The slow recovery

However, out of the hardship and confusion, a new and dynamic economy began to emerge. The recovery, though slow, was largely due to the new ideas and technologies that had been developing throughout the world since the beginning of the century.

The chemical industry made great strides forward during the 1920s and 1930s. Artificial fertilizers and pesticides were developing and these were very important. These chemicals enabled farmers to grow more crops on their land and thus helped the world economy. This period also saw the industrial development of numerous different types of plastic materials. Early in the century a Belgian scientist, Leo Baekeland, had cre-ated a new material which he called Bakelite. This was widely used in the 1920s and 1930s, but it was hard and brittle. It was soon to be replaced by other plastics developed by Du Pont in the USA and Imperial Chemical Industries in Britain. These companies developed polythene and PVC materials, replacing wood and metal in many uses.

Electronic equipment was also steadily gaining ground. More and more homes were being equipped with electricity through the mains. This meant that there was a large market for such goods as vacuum cleaners, heaters, lights and other household equipment. Throughout this period domestic appliances improved rapidly in design and range. By 1939 most homes were equipped with a variety of electrical gadgets.

Below An American fuel pump factory with a central conveyor belt. After the Depression, there was plenty of work as trade slowly recovered.

Above The use of machinery and chemicals on farm land increased food production and helped industry.

Left Sacks of cocoa beans being handled at Cadbury's chocolate factory in Birmingham, England.

Right An advert-
isement for the 1934
Ford V8 saloon. The
motor industry was
thriving at this time.
The Ford factory at
Dagenham, Essex was
the most modern in the
industry.

V-8 SALOON DE LUXE (4 DOORS), NEWLY REDUCED PRICE, £235, AT WORKS, DAGENHAM

Do you like to *more* when you sit behind the wheel of a car? Then drive the V-8 just once.
From a standing start you reach forty—almost imperceptibly. Slip into top—put your foot
down . . . never in your motoring life have you had such a thrill, such a sense of power,
speed and safety.
Go to the nearest Ford dealer. Sit behind the wheel of the V-8. Get the "feel" of it yourself,
and see at how reasonable a cost the greatest thrill in modern motoring can be yours for
thousands of miles to come.

Power and transport

Industry also made great use of this new
power. Rather than have a bulky steam
engine producing power for machines,
many factory owners preferred to use
electrical energy. This led to a decline in
the factory use of coal but a rise in the
consumption of electricity.

The motor trade was also booming at
this time. Hundreds of thousands of cars
and trucks were being produced. The
road haulage industry grew from virtually
nothing to dominate transport by 1939.
Most goods left their factories on lorries,
or by railway container. This caused a

rising demand for new vehicles and for repair facilities, both of which created job opportunities.

Worldwide a new pattern was also emerging. In place of the pre-war situation where only parts of Europe and North America were industrialized, the years between the wars saw a rise in industry elsewhere. Indian industrial output trebled during this period. This was due to the fact that India assumed a large share of the cotton industry, which in turn provided capital for the development of other industries. Japan took the process a stage further. Beginning with textiles, Japanese industry developed rapidly to include steel foundries, shipyards and one of the most modern industries of the time – the manufacture of aeroplanes.

By 1936, the aircraft industry was well established in Europe and the USA, and air routes were linking the main cities of the world. Germany, also, had airliners and airships, and was re-emerging as a world power. It was clear that another world war would soon take place.

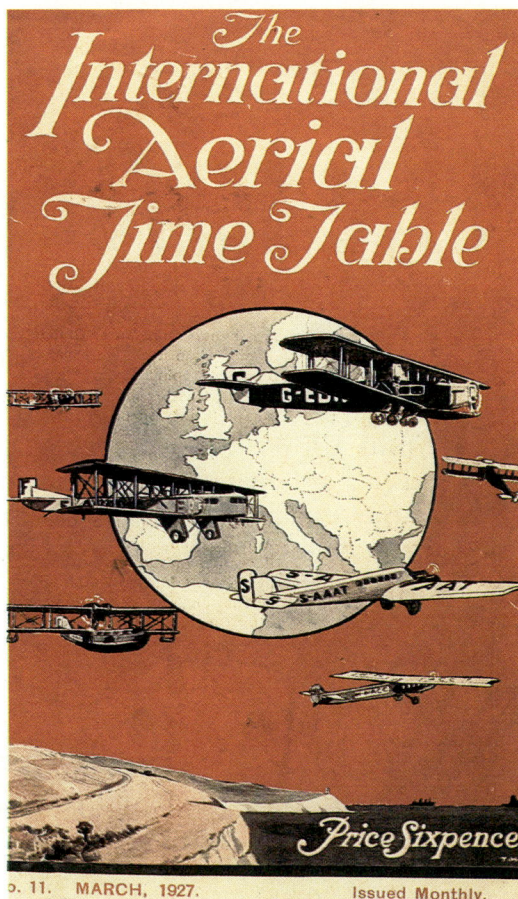

The
International Aerial Time Table

Price Sixpence

o. 11.   MARCH, 1927.   Issued Monthly.

Left *By the late 1920s, many airlines were operating regular passenger flights between major cities. International air travel had arrived.*

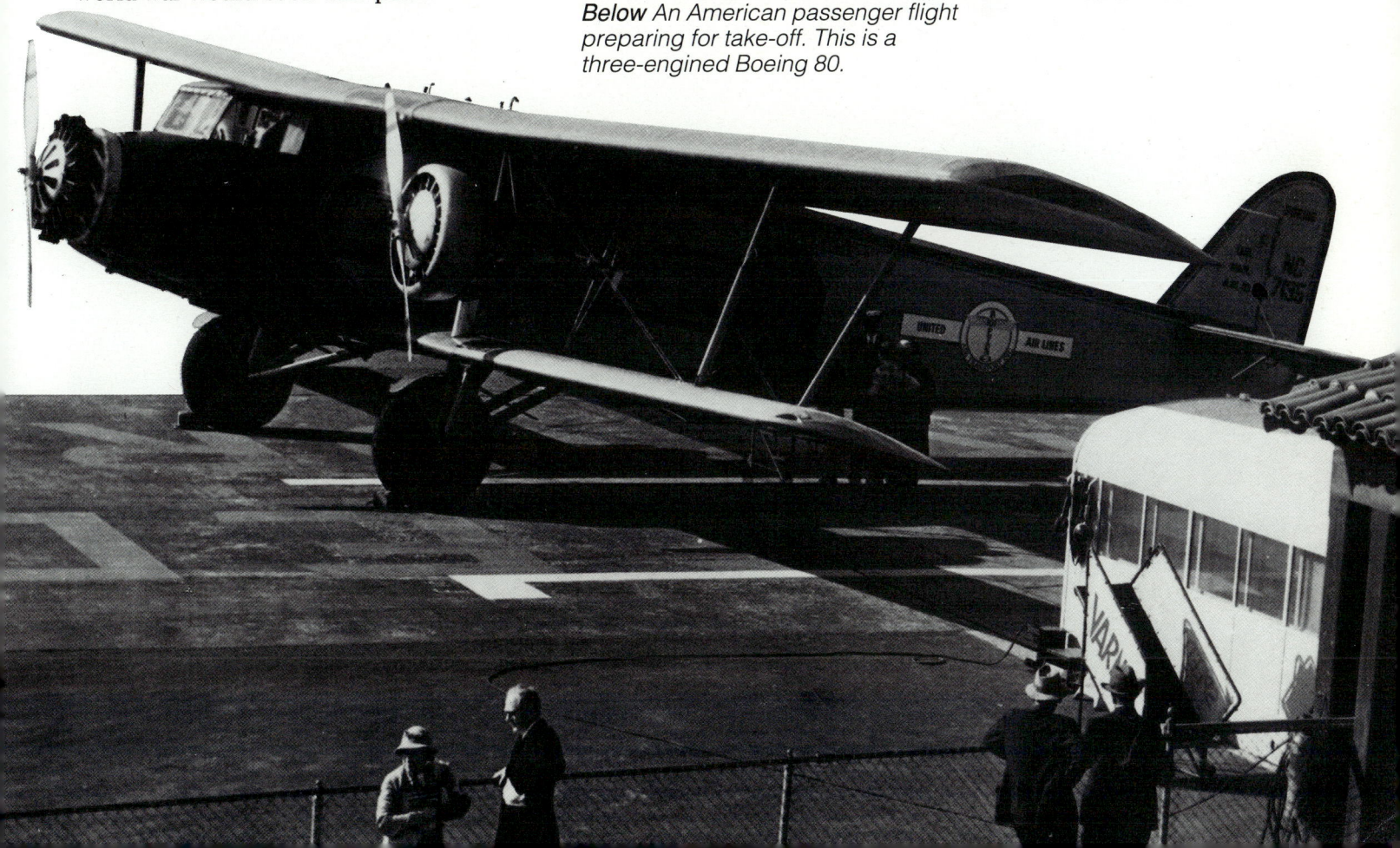

Below *An American passenger flight preparing for take-off. This is a three-engined Boeing 80.*

The Effects of War

By the mid-1930s world industry and trade were slowly improving but were handicapped by changes in international finance. Before the First World War most countries had tied their currencies to gold, so that monetary units had a set value in gold. This allowed for easy conversion from one currency to another.

A time of uncertainty

Below As the Second World War approached, many nations increased production of weapons. This factory was built in 1937 to produce aircraft engines for the British Royal Air Force.

During the slump, the gold standard had been abandoned resulting in confusion and inflation, and many countries placed restrictions on trade and the flow of finance. As a result, countries found it difficult to buy from abroad. This helped home industry to some degree but hindered the re-establishment of a world trading pattern such as had existed before the First World War.

In the late 1930s it became clear that Germany was acting aggressively and was intent on war. This resulted in increased spending on defence in many countries, including aircraft manufacture, engineering and shipbuilding. For Europe and the USA it was a short period of prosperity and uncertainty.

CYLINDER HEAD LINE

The Second World War

At the outbreak of war in 1939 governments acted quickly to reimpose controls. In Britain, the government acquired powers to control all industries essential to the war effort. These included shipbuilding, munitions, aircraft construction and most forms of engineering. Car manufacturers were soon making military vehicles and tanks. Bicycle manufacturers, such as B.S.A. (Birmingham Small Arms), Raleigh and Hercules, had to limit the output of cycles and manufactured machine guns and aircraft components.

During the war scientists and engineers created and perfected numerous inventions, including radar. Improvements in radio equipment and the radar installations greatly aided the war effort. When the war was over these advances helped a number of new industries to expand in peacetime conditions. As we shall see later, the jet engine, invented during the war, was to have a huge effect on the aeroplane industry. The German secret weapons, the V1 and the V2, used new rocket technology. After the end of the war, German scientists helped the American and Russian space projects.

Rationing and repair

The British government also imposed strict rationing on food, clothing and other goods. This was designed to ensure a fair distribution of essential goods in a beleaguered island. At this time a new line of utility clothing was introduced, designed to use as little material and labour as possible.

When the war ended, rationing in Britain remained for several years. This was

done in order to stop people spending too much money on foreign goods and to give British industry time to recover from war damage. At the same time the government nationalized many industries, including coal, gas, electricity and long-distance road haulage. During the war, shipyards, factories and homes had been destroyed by bombing, and a massive rebuilding programme took place. Factories started turning out prefabricated buildings, known as 'prefabs', and these helped to solve the housing shortage in Britain.

The war against Japan had been brought to a close by the dropping of two atomic bombs on the Japanese homeland. The work carried out by the atomic scientists was soon to be converted to peaceful rather than destructive ends in the form of nuclear power stations.

Above Dr Wernher von Braun (centre), German rocket scientist, who helped the USA in the postwar years to develop the space programme.

Below In 1949 this was the 'kitchen of tomorrow'.

'You've Never Had it so Good'

In 1959 the British Prime Minister, Harold Macmillan, told the public, 'You've never had it so good'. In many ways he was right, for the years between 1950 and 1970 were ones of rapid growth and development in industry. Many new inventions came into use and prosperity blossomed as never before. Many trends which had begun in the 1940s continued and expanded as the modern industrial scene came into being.

Growth and prosperity

The keynote of the era was the increase in demand for consumer goods. As people became increasingly wealthy through employment and wage rises, they demanded more home comforts and conveniences. Electrical equipment for the home became increasingly common and sophisticated. During the war, for instance, very few households had a fridge, but by 1962 more than a third of homes had one. A similar boom occurred in television ownership. Also on the increase was the demand for such products as radios, food mixers, record players and other domestic appliances.

Far right A 1957 portable transistor radio which was made to fit jacket pockets and weighed less than 600 grams.

Right Harold Macmillan, who was British Prime Minister from 1957 to 1963.

This demand was met by a growing industry which concentrated on mass production and mechanization. This in turn created a demand for sophisticated equipment which stimulated the engineering business. The electronics industry continually strove to make its products smaller and cheaper. One of the greatest advances was the development of the transistor by Dr. William Shockley at the Bell Telephone Laboratories in the USA. This tiny component replaced the bulky valves on which many pieces of equipment had previously relied.

The transistor allowed electrical equipment to be made smaller, more cheaply and in greater quantities. Many industries came to rely on transistors to a large extent. Electronic equipment could be used to perform automatically tasks that had previously used bulky and expensive mechanical devices.

The motor trade became increasingly important. Mass-produced cars, taking advantage of the latest automated machinery, were now produced at prices which many people could afford. The great increase in motor traffic caused governments to build bigger and better roads. Britain's first motorway was opened in 1959. Better roads led to more goods being moved by lorry. The motor industry continually made improvements to their products and to their factories. Many of the innovations in factory production and management had their origin in the motor industry.

Above A British cotton mill in 1960. Textiles continued to decline in the postwar era, as the countries of the Far East captured the markets.

Left These airtight jars contain hundreds of tiny transistors. These took the place of bulky valves and transformed the radio industry.

Right Carnaby Street, London, which became the colourful centre for new fashions and new ideas in consumer goods.

Below Japanese workers assembling combined 'lighter-cameras' for export to the USA and other countries.

New ideas

The chemical industry continued to expand in many fields. Artificial fibres, such as nylon and polyester, came into common use. Ladies stockings and men's shirts were made from nylon, which allowed them to be both cheaper and thinner than cotton equivalents. As time passed, the textile industry started to mix artificial fibres with wool and cotton to create a whole range of new materials which combined the advantages of both. Darning socks and starching shirts became a thing of the past.

New and improved medicines were also produced by the chemical industry. These might be for home use, in the treatment of headaches or small cuts, or for professional use.

Sulphur drugs, in particular, greatly aided the fight against disease. They controlled many illnesses and saved countless lives. Vaccinations also became much more effective. Some diseases, such as polio, were almost eradicated by these new drugs. Chemical fertilizers and selective pesticides were constantly being improved to help farmers. In more advanced countries these allowed intensive farming, producing large amounts of food from small areas of land.

The rapid development of aircraft design which took place during the Second World War had by now totally revolutionized civil aviation and the aircraft industry as a whole. Within a few short years most major cities of the world were linked by regular passenger air flights. The invention of the jet engine greatly aided this process. The first jet passenger aircraft was the de Havilland Comet which came into service in 1952 with a flight from London to Johannesburg, South Africa. This was followed by the Boeing 707 and in 1969 by the jumbo jet.

Above A traffic jam on the newly-opened M1 motorway in Northamptonshire. Note the cars in the lay-by, broken down due to overheating.

Left Inside the packaging department of a chemical factory. At this time plastics were beginning to be widely used for packaging and for protective clothing.

The expansion of world trade

This increase of air travel had a marked effect on world trade. People were able to visit countries many hundreds of miles from their own. Business people were also able to deal directly with their international customers. Instead of a ship voyage or lengthy correspondence, a British businessman could be in New York in just a few hours to meet his customers face to face. This had the general effect of increasing international trade and improving international co-operation.

While most of the developed countries concentrated on consumer goods and high technology industries, the growing affluence of the world had its effect in Asia and the Third World. Japan recovered quickly from its defeat in 1945 and rebuilt industry rapidly, so becoming a major manufacturing country. Other places in

Asia, such as Hong Kong and Taiwan, were also beginning to industrialize, though even by 1970 this was still on a fairly small scale.

Many areas in Africa and South America began to develop some form of industry. On the whole, these remained tied to agricultural or mineral products of the country. Copper mining in Zambia, for instance, dominated the industry of that country. This led to increased prosperity, but left the countries vulnerable to serious setbacks when demand for their product declined.

One sphere of industry which was to be important for the future was energy production. Throughout the 1950s and 1960s energy consumption soared. In 1972 demand per head of population was more than double what it was in 1950.

Some of this increase was due to domestic energy needs, such as central heating, but most demand came from transport and industry. By 1970 oil and gas provided twice as much energy as coal. The new sources of energy, such as hydroelectricity and nuclear power, were only just beginning to be used. The trade and economy of most nations depended vitally upon oil and its by-products.

Left Widespread use of combine harvesters on farms increased crop yields, but cut the number of jobs for farm workers.

Below One of the first Boeing 747s. These jumbo jets have enabled many more people to enjoy cheap air travel than ever before.

The Oil Crisis

By 1970 the industrial face of the world had changed greatly. The old staple industries had been partly superseded by new industries based on new inventions and discoveries. The industrial wealth of the world was spread wider than in 1900, though still rather unevenly. However, changes were to come quickly and dramatically.

Right A major oil refinery in Kuwait, an Arab nation that produces large amounts of crude oil.

The price of prosperity

One of the first signs was when inflation began to rise. In most industrialized countries money became worth less than before. In 1973 in Italy the rate of value loss, known as inflation, was over 10 per cent. In Britain inflation ran at about 9 per cent. Such variations disturbed international trade, but governments were able to deal with the problems.

Then in 1974 the price of oil soared. This was largely due to the actions of OPEC (Organization of Petroleum-Exporting Countries), which included most nations of the Middle East. They believed that they were not receiving enough money from oil sales to allow them to develop other industries. There also seemed to be a wish to demonstrate the power which these governments held over the world's economy. OPEC therefore quadrupled the price of oil. This caused equally sharp increases in the price of petrol, lubricating oil and other oil-based products.

Left During the oil crisis, new cars continued to be manufactured, but sales dropped and stocks quickly built up at the factories.

Below Inside a modern paper mill. The machine only needs one supervisor but it consumes a large amount of energy.

The energy crisis

This had an immediate effect on the world economy. Poor nations, in the early stages of industrialization, were hit hardest. They went into debt as they tried to pay the higher price for oil and still maintain their growth. The heavily industrialized countries also suffered. Energy formed a large part of the raw-material cost for industry. The enormous jump in oil prices caused increases in nearly all other prices as well. In Britain prices rose by 24 per cent in 1975. This added to the

Top A petrol station in Britain closes as it runs out of petrol during the oil crisis.

Left Sheikh Yamani, the Arab spokesman for OPEC. In 1975, despite the rise in oil prices, over 3 million barrels of oil per day were being sold by OPEC to countries around the world.

existing problems to cause very high inflation. Industrial output fell and the world economy began to slow down.

The crisis had an unexpected effect. While some oil-producing countries became very rich, others suffered from the general economic slow-down. In 1979, OPEC demanded a second steep rise in oil prices. Though this temporarily solved their own problems, it created more for the world at large. Those poor countries already in debt found they could not pay for the loans. This led to a serious debt-crisis which is still in existence. Richer countries suffered a fall in industrial activity. Factories closed and people were put out of work. For the first time, the value of industrial output in most countries actually fell.

Despite the problems caused by the energy crisis, industry continued to become more efficient. The trends already seen before 1970 continued.

Meanwhile, the electronics industry had been expanding in many countries. The expansion was based on the earlier development of very small components. This industry would soon change again.

Below Inside a sugar refinery in Mauritius. At the time of the oil crisis, factories requiring large amounts of electricity had to shut down.

The shaping of the modern world

The silicon chip came into widespread use after it was developed for use in the US space programme. The chip made possible even further miniaturization of electronic equipment. Before 1970, computers had been bulky, delicate instruments which filled large areas of office space and demanded careful temperature control. By 1980 the first pocket calcula- tors were for sale in high street shops.

The aircraft industry continued to ad- vance as new wide-bodied jet airliners came into use. Sophisticated radar and tracking equipment was produced which made air travel both safer and cheaper. Despite the setback caused by the in- creased cost of oil products and raw materials, the European and American

Below The Anglo-French Concorde, the first supersonic passenger airliner.

Right Early office computers were large and bulky, but they greatly assisted in the storage of stock records, and in invoicing.

chemical industries continued to grow in efficiency and usefulness. This lead was followed by many industries in the developed world. Mechanization and automation continued to gain ground, cutting costs and increasing profitability. This resulted in some unemployment, but in higher wages and better working conditions for those who remained in steady employment.

Some industries, such as shipbuilding and textiles, moved away from wealthy countries towards less industrialized areas. The lower wages and development costs to be found in poorer countries was a great attraction and places such as Taiwan and Korea found themselves experiencing a boom in industrial growth. The industrial picture of the world was changing rapidly.

Above Robots are controlled by computers. This one is seen handling a washing machine, an unwieldy job for human workers.

Into the Computer Age

Throughout the 1970s computers had been becoming cheaper and more widely used. Since 1980 they have had an increasingly important role in many industries. This has been achieved by continued research into design and programming. The development of the integrated circuit on the silicon chip and of magnetic information systems has made computers smaller, faster and more powerful.

Below Inside the rolling mill of an American aluminium factory. The coils of sheet are wound rapidly onto rolls and the process is computer-controlled. The rolled aluminium sheeting is used in aircraft manufacture.

Computers in industry

In the motor industry, computers are used to control robots which are pro-grammed to carry out repetitive tasks previously done by hand. This has greatly improved efficiency in car factories. Other industries were quick to follow the

lead and installed robots. Today many industries use robotic systems to carry out difficult manufacturing processes.

It is not only in factories that computers have had an effect. Many small businesses use computers to help with accounts and records thereby simplifying their office procedures. The ability of computers to store and update information on disk has enabled banks and others to give their customers improved services. In the preparation of newspapers and books, word processors are widely used in the editorial processes.

The transport industry is now vitally dependent on computers. They are used to control movement and safety, whether on land, at sea or in the air.

Below A technical expert designing a robot for a precision task. She is using a system known as computer-assisted design, or CAD.

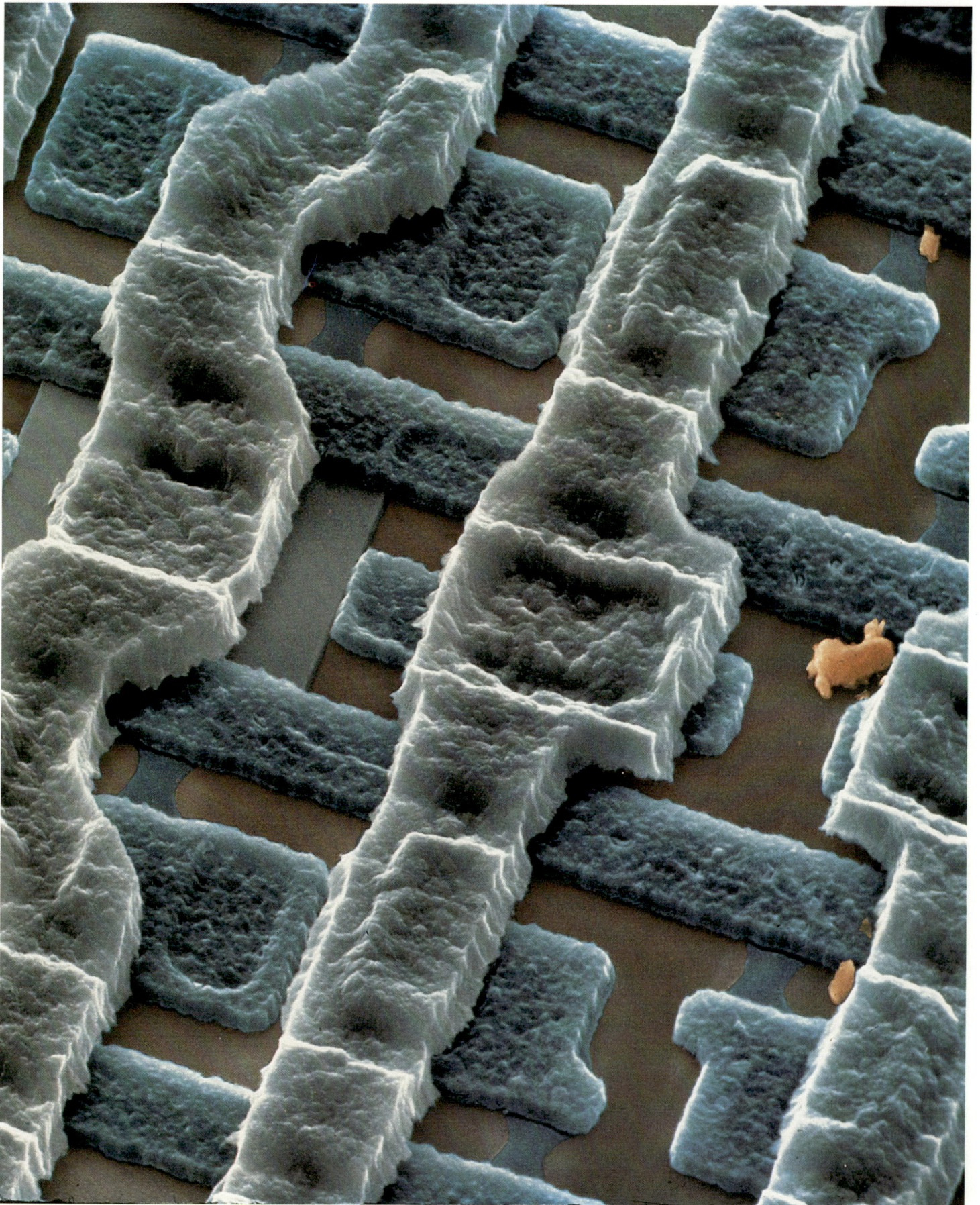

Communications

Industrialized countries all have a part to play in the communications industry. Communication satellites are in constant orbit around the Earth. Some of these help predict the weather or relay telephone messages, others have military uses. These satellites have only been made possible by the production of miniaturized computers.

The recent development of fibre optics is also opening up new communication possibilities. Far more signals can be carried along a fibre-optic channel than along an electric cable. This should greatly aid telephone and computer communications, by reducing the cost of transmitting messages, though not all the problems of fibre optics have yet been solved by scientists.

One of the most recent discoveries with promise for the future is that of superconductors. These are metals which have no electrical resistance at certain temperatures. Hitherto, such superconductors would only work at certain temperatures far below freezing point. Now, however, alloys have been found that are superconductors at close to room temperature, which opens up many new possibilities for electronics.

Opposite A silicon integrated circuit, magnified hundreds of times. The orange particles are impurities.

Below Many aspects of office work, such as letter writing, filing and keeping records, have been greatly simplified by the use of word processors and small computers.

The world today

In recent years the dependence of the world on fossil fuels, such as coal and oil, has been slightly reduced by the introduction of nuclear power stations. Although these do not create atmospheric pollution (except in the case of accidents such as occurred at Chernobyl, USSR, in 1986) as do other power stations, they do produce dangerous radioactive waste. The safe disposal of this waste is itself becoming a new industry.

Industry in the developed countries has become increasingly sophisticated and the trend has generally been beneficial, providing improved living standards and increased opportunities. Sadly, there are still countries, such as Bangladesh and Ethiopia, where living standards are desperately low, and where famine and disasters create death and starvation. Perhaps in the future, industry will become so efficient that a wider and fairer spread of its benefits will be available to the less fortunate.

Above Fibre optics, by which signals pass along a glass fibre at the speed of light, is a new science. These thin fibres will replace electric cables.

Far Left
A communications satellite is placed in orbit by the American Space Shuttle.

43

Above Even plastic can be beautiful as the picture shows.

Glossary

Alloy A metal that is made by mixing two or more different metals together.

Artificial fibre A fibre that is man-made rather than natural.

Automation The use of machines in a factory to do work needing little or no human control.

Bakelite The first plastic material to be made from chemicals. Bakelite can only be made in dark colours.

Bankrupt Unable to pay debts. A person, company or country can become bankrupt.

Boom A state of affairs when business is good. A boom is the opposite of a slump.

Cash crop A crop which people grow to sell, and not to use themselves. Several countries grow tea as a cash crop.

Communication satellite An artificial satellite in orbit around the Earth used to relay radio, television and telephone signals.

Component Any one part of several that go to make up a finished product. A pedal is one of several bicycle components.

Consumer goods Goods that are produced or manufactured to satisfy human needs.

Depression A state of affairs when national or international trade and prosperity is in a severely reduced condition.

Economy The strength of a country's trade, industry and money supply.

Fertilizer A chemical that is added to the soil to make plants and crops grow better.

Fibre optics A technology that deals with the passage of light along very fine glass fibres. Fibre-optic cables are used to pass radio, television and telephone signals.

High technology An advanced, sophisticated technology in a specialist field such as electronics.

Inflation A continuing increase in the level of prices.

Integrated circuit A complicated electrical circuit made up as a complete system in a single silicon chip.

Intensive farming Getting as much produce as possible from an area of land.

Internal combustion A process in which energy is released to drive a piston by burning a mixture of fuel and air inside a cylinder.

Investment Laying out money so as to develop industry and thereby make profit.

Man-made fibre An artificial fibre created by chemical processes to take the place of a natural fibre.

Manufacture To make by hand or with the help of machines.

Mass production The manufacture of any goods in very large quantities, using the same process and machinery, over and over again.

Miniaturization Making something in the smallest size possible, such as an electrical circuit on a silicon chip.

Nationalize To make an industry the property of the nation, and to bring it under national management.

Nylon A very strong plastic substance used in the manufacture of textiles, ropes and other goods. It was developed by scientists working in New York and London, hence its name.

Pesticide Any chemical substance that kills pests. An insecticide kills insects, and a fungicide kills fungi.

Plastics These are man-made materials that can be moulded into shape, made into film or into thread. Many of them are formed from oil products.

Polythene A transparent plastic film that is made from oil. It is widely used for packaging food.

Prefabrication Making something, such as a house or garage, that can be put together later.

Production line A line in a factory along which a product can be assembled by the work force in easy stages.

Profit The gain, or difference between the selling price and the total cost of the product being sold.

PVC Polyvinyl chloride, a flexible plastic material used instead of rubber to coat electric wires.

Radar Radar is short for **r**adio **d**etecting **a**nd **r**anging. Radio waves are bounced off an object and their return is timed to calculate the distance of the object from the origin of the radio waves.

Radioactive Describes heavy elements, such as uranium or radium, which give off harmful rays, or radiation.

Rationing Fixing by law the allowance of commodities in short supply, such as food, clothing, water or petrol.

Raw materials Materials, often in their raw or natural state such as coal or iron, from which goods are manufactured.

Research The detailed study needed to advance the state of knowledge in any subject.

Robot A machine that can be programmed and designed to do tasks that are normally done by people.

Silicon chip A thin, very small disc of silicon with one or more electrical circuits etched on to it.

Slump A state of affairs when business is bad. A slump is the opposite of a boom.

Staple industry A settled and leading industry in a country. At one time coffee was the staple industry of Brazil.

Superconductor A metal or alloy which shows a complete loss of electrical resistance at a certain temperature.

Technology The application and practical use of science in industry.

Textiles Woven fabrics, both of natural and man-made fibres.

Transistor A small electronic valve through which an electric current flows at a controlled rate. A transistor can increase the strength of an electric signal.

Further Reading

Ashworth, W., **A Short History of the International Economy since 1850** (Longman, 1987).

Burgess, J., **People and Energy** (Macmillan, 1988).

Clarke, D., **The Encyclopedia of How it Works** (Marshall Cavendish, 1978).

Dineen, J., **Twenty Inventors** (Wayland, 1988).

Lambert, M., **Future Sources of Energy** (Wayland, 1986).

Marwick, A., **Britain in our Century** (Thames and Hudson, 1984).

Piper, A., **Oil** (Franklin Watts, 1980).

Pizzey, S., and Snowden, S., **The Computerized Society** (Wayland, 1986).

Storrs, G., **The Robot Age** (Wayland, 1986).

Picture acknowledgements

The illustrations in this book were supplied by: BBC Hulton Picture Library 18; British Telecommunications 43; The Mansell Collection 19 (above); Science Photo Library 40; Topham 4, 5, 6, 7 (above), 8 (below), 9 (below), 10, 11 (below), 12 (both), 13 (both), 15 (below), 16, 17, 19 (below), 20, 21 (below), 22, 23, 24 (above), 25 (both), 26 (both), 27 (both), 28 (both), 29 (below), 31 (both), 32, 33 (above), 34 (both), 36 (both), 38, 42; TRH (The Research House) 8 (above), 9 (above), 11 (above), 14, 15 (above), 21 (above), 39, 41; ZEFA *frontispiece*, 24 (below), 29 (above), 30, 33 (below), 35, 37, 44.

Index